This book Copyright © 1990 by Wise Publications,
A Division of Music Sales Corporation, New York, NY.

Order No. AM 81316
US International Standard Book Number: 0.8256.1292.6
UK International Standard Book Number: 0.7119.2376.0

Exclusive Distributors:
Music Sales Corporation
225 Park Avenue South, New York, NY 10003 USA
Music Sales Limited
8/9 Frith Street, London W1V 5TZ England
Music Sales Pty. Limited
120 Rothschild Street, Rosebery, Sydney, NSW 2018,
Australia

Designed by: Kay Shuckhart
Photo Research: Amanda Rubin

Printed in the United States of America by
Vicks Lithograph and Printing Corporation

PHOTO CREDITS

Cover: Laura Levine
Backcover: Laura Levine
Poster: Barry Morgenstein/Retna, Ltd.
(page 1) George DuBose; (2-3) Laura Levine; (4-5) Curtis Knapp
/G.D.; (6) Geoffrey Croft/Retna, Ltd.; (7) Nick Elgar/London
Features International; Jeffrey Mayer; (8) George DuBose;
(9) London Features International; (10) George DuBose; (11)
Kees Tabak/Retna, Ltd.; (12-13) George DuBose; (14) Curtis
Knapp/G.D.; (16) George DuBose; (18-19) George DuBose;
(20) Randy Bauer/Ron Gallela, Ltd.; (21) John Barrett/
lobe Photos; (22) Laura Levine; (23) Adrian Boot/Retna,
Ltd.; (24) A.J. Barratt; (25) Laura Levine; (26-27) Laura
Levine; (28-29) George DuBose; (30) George DuBose; (31)
Jeffery Mayer, Susan Martin/AMFAR; (32) George DuBose.

"We are a big favorite among two-year-olds." / *Kate Pierson*

"We have this special pipeline, back entrance pipeline, to the subconscious that no one else has discovered. A lot comes from that." / *Fred Schneider*

"It's been a cosmic kind of day, I'm telling you." / *Kate Pierson*

"There's a real participation with us and the audience. We get a lot of energy from them and we give it back. It completes a circle." / *Kate Pierson*

i

It all began rather innocently in Athens, Georgia, a town known for poultry processing and college keg parties, when Keith Strickland befriended Ricky Wilson in high school at the beginning of the '70s. Ricky had a little two-track home recorder and a trunk full of impressive if somewhat unformed songs, and soon the two began collaborating on material.

In many ways, Athens is a perfect example of a small southern town, but the presence of the University of Georgia and the subsequent youth influx provides a fertile atmosphere for creativity and other sorts of deviant behavior. Unlike many comparable small cities, Athens has always enjoyed (or endured, depending on your point of view) the influence of an active lunatic fringe. But in the B-52's' day, there was no real music scene. Bands like R.E.M., which also came from Athens, were still a glimmer in their parents' . . . something or other.

Ricky and Keith were enthusiastic members of this particular "In Crowd" and spent most of their time together, hanging out, playing in garage bands, and experimenting with their wardrobes and the tolerance level of Athens' more conservative elements. Longtime friend Robert Waldrop, who has contributed lyrics to some of the B-52's' songs, reconstructed a vintage Keith Strickland getup for the benefit of *Spin* magazine: ". . . He had really long hair and it was all teased out, and a shiny silver jacket, and high black boots." The effect was completed with a truck mirror affixed for the ultimate big-jewelry statement . . . and this was Keith's choice of day wear!

And then along came Fred Schneider, a native of the sunny surfin' Jersey Shore. Mr. Schneider went south to tame the wild trees, but his stint as a forestry major led him straight off the garden path and into the woods. It seems that Fred also possessed a passion for dancing the night away in oddball ensembles. His special fashion tip at the time involved a car-sick mixture of clashing colors, and it wasn't uncommon to spot him (from at least a mile

off) displaying some interesting combination of lime green, orange, purple, and brown. The colorful Mr. Schneider eventually swapped forestry for journalism when he was required to chop down a tree (and you thought you had a problem with homework).

It was only a matter of time before the three guys joined forces, and soon they were jamming together. Ricky and Keith would play whatever they could lay their hands on and Fred babbled about whatever he felt like babbling about.

In the middle of the "Me" decade, recent Athens immigrant Kate Pierson was busy teaching the '70s what the '60s were all about. She was playing in a folk band called the Sun Donuts, working in her garden and rearing ingrate goats who rewarded her tender care by walking all over her car.

Meanwhile, the rest of the future '52's dallied with the tedium of de rigueur, pre-stardom day jobs. Fred served time in the Bluebird Cafe and dished up twenty-nine flavors of tofu lentils in the Eldorado vegetarian restaurant. Keith and Ricky walked the Greyhound at the local bus station (which was run by Ma and Pa Strickland), and Ricky's little sis Cindy slung shakes at the fabulously monikered Whirly-Q Luncheonette.

The official story of their initial communion centers around a local liquid delicacy served at the neighborhood Chinese eatery. After partaking of a giant, fiery libation aptly named a Flaming Volcano, the quintet stumbled and giggled their way over to a friend's house with nothing more on their stir-fried minds than a spirited bash on his array of instruments. Everyone had a great time, and a band was born. They began to play together regularly, sometimes in a deserted embalming room of a funeral parlor that provided a fertile garden for their growing identity.

Fred, wearing Kate's "martian hat," has replaced the traditional
"book on the head" with a cocktail and can still
maintain perfect poise.

Boogie-meister Schneider admonishing his dancing partner
for getting out of step. Definite no-no!

Cindy, during "Give Me Back My Man,"
enthralls the Max's Kansas City audience that
contained Brian Eno and Robert Fripp.

Kate and Cindy, in the basement of the Mudd
Club, adding final touches to their perfect-dos.

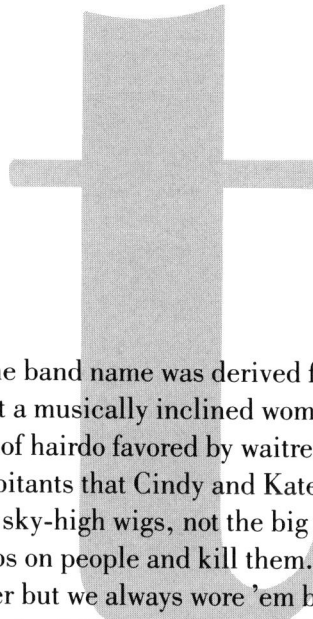

The band name was derived from a dream Keith had about a musically inclined woman with a big bouffant, the kind of hairdo favored by waitresses and trailer-park inhabitants that Cindy and Kate take to the limit with their sky-high wigs, not the big nasty planes that drop bombs on people and kill them. "The wigs have become bigger but we always wore 'em before we started the band, at parties," Kate told Toby Goldstein. "The big thing was to go to the Potter's House, the thrift store, and find an old, ratty wig. Sometimes we'd find a good one and two people would tear at it and get it all knotty. Sometimes we'd put two wigs on top of each other and a high heel on the very top. That made a very festive atmosphere."

Putting hair wear aside for the moment, the B-52's were inspired by a need to banish any hint of boredom. "Part of the reason we started the band was because you had to create your own entertainment," Kate explains. "Especially at the beginning, the one idea we did have was that we wanted to be a dance band," Keith adds. "We haven't thought about it too much since then, now that we've got this momentum. It's just how we write."

From the beginning, composition was a group effort, with Keith and Ricky penning the tunes, and Kate, Cindy, and Fred concocting their own special brand of funny, cryptic lyrics. The first single, "Rock Lobster," was inspired in a rather roundabout way by an evening Fred spent in a pathetic disco in Atlanta, whose idea of a fab light show was a rotational display of slides featuring kids and dogs and other suburban wonderama, including a cooked you-know-what. Somehow, the title "Rock Lobster" just appealed to him. After Keith and Ricky came up with a tune and Kate and Cindy added their distinctive, piercing vocals, it became a perfect tune to trot out at their debut "gig."

The band premiered at an otherwise run-of-the-mill Valentine's Day party. Their friends and acquaintances went berserk and pulled out their coolest dance moves as the B-52's bombarded them with early versions of "Dance This Mess Around," "Rock Lobster," and other perennial faves that later surfaced on the first album. "I threw my

leg out," Robert Waldrop said in *Spin* magazine. "That was a good dance party."

After a successful stint of entertaining themselves and every other hipster in the immediate vicinity, the B's took advantage of a road trip to New York City with pals from Atlanta, The Fans, to leave a tape with the booking agent at Max's Kansas City. At the time, Max's and CBGB's were basically the only game in town for new bands, so it was fortunate that they appreciated the band's sound.

On December 12, 1977, the B-52's played Max's for the first time. Prevailing conditions, economic and otherwise, had left most New York clubbers and clubbettes rather sluggish, and there were about twenty people in the audience, including employees. Nonetheless, an offer for a return engagement was proffered and accepted, and soon the band began commuting north of the Mason-Dixon line regularly, generating their own little buzz downtown.

Though many critics and musicians praised the B's, mainstream audience response to their gigs at Max's and CBGB's varied severely. Jane Errhed, a frequent Max's attendee, remembers an early gig: "I think it was right before 'Rock Lobster' came out, and there was a rumor going around that there were two drag queens in the band, which helped stir up people's curiosity. The place was completely packed, and almost nobody was dancing. You have to realize that it wasn't really considered good form at the time in NYC to even acknowledge the fact that there was a band onstage, so their attempts to generate a 'party spirit' totally went against the prevailing winds of the time, which sort of demanded a lot of slouching and rolling of eyeballs." The hostile environment didn't exactly inspire the Georgians, who were used to feeding off their audiences' energy. "They weren't very good," Jane adds. "They also didn't know that everyone in NYC played really short sets back then, and it seemed like they were onstage for about a year! But the next time I saw them, a few years later at the Mudd Club, they were immeasurably improved, even though they were assaulted by a giant lobster."

Cindy remembers the giant lobster incident well: "That was the silliest guy in the world! We warned him not to do it, but he jumps onstage during 'Rock Lobster' and everything caves in and there's a big hole (in the stage)

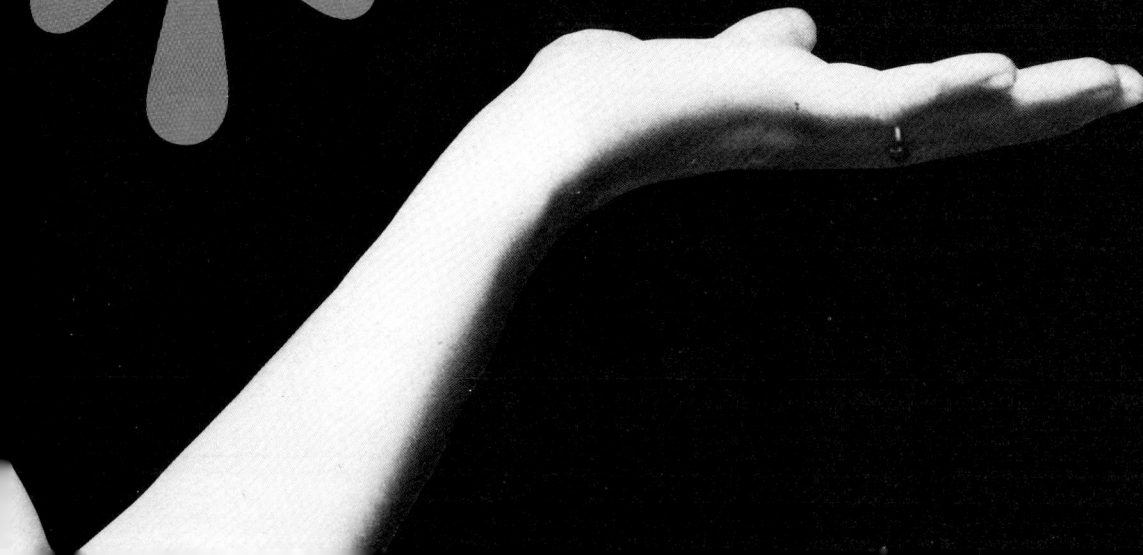

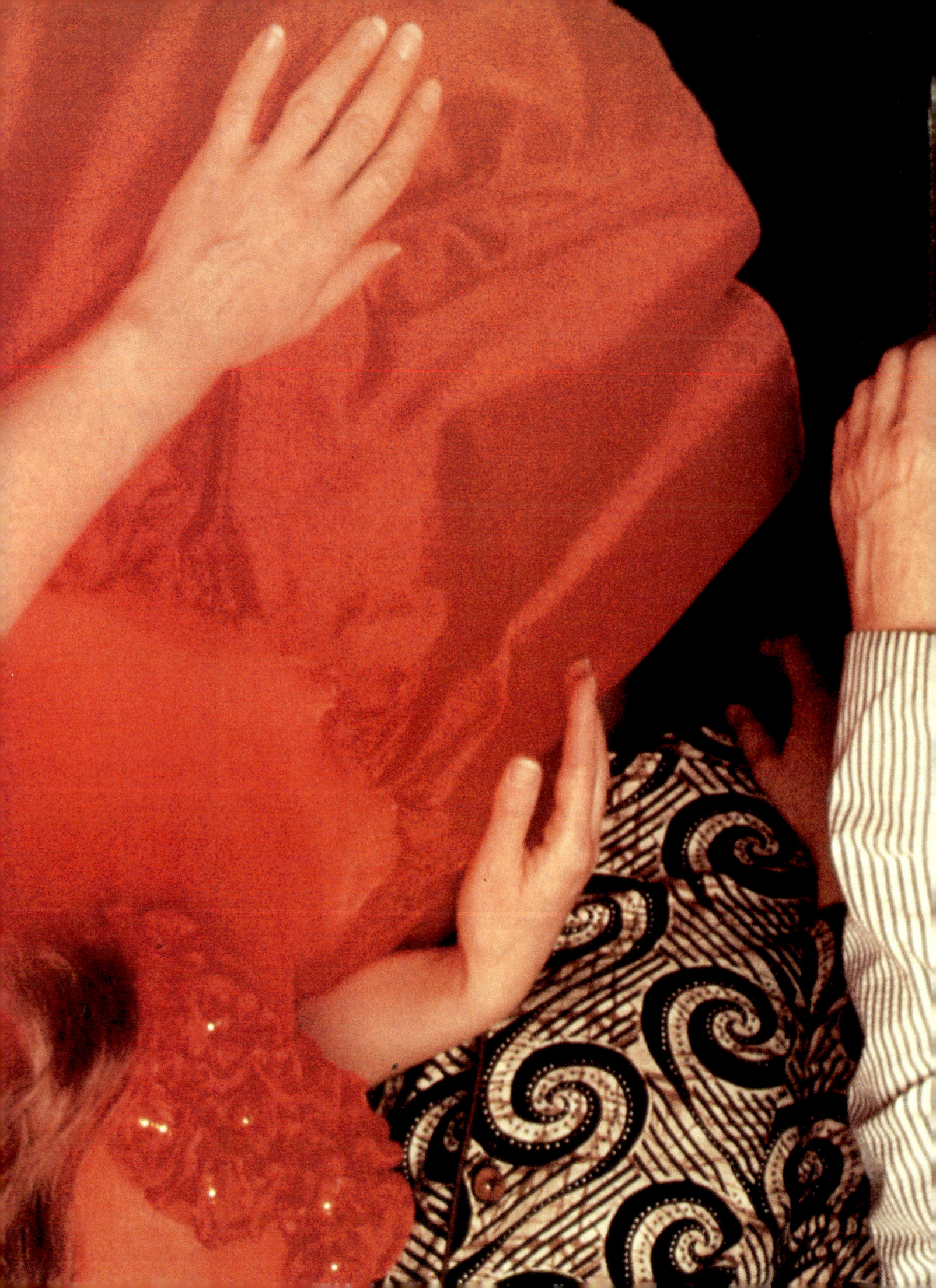

and the drums start sinking in. And that night Frank Zappa and William Burroughs were there." For years after, a B-52's' show could turn into Night of the Living Lobsters at the flick of a barnacled claw. "We'll go play somewhere and there'll be lots of people with those plastic lobster hats . . . They've got these big crustacean legs on 'em. I see them chasing me in my sleep."

At the end of the day, a dash of ballot-stuffing didn't hurt those early B-52's' shows. "We cheated a lot," Cindy confessed in *Spin* magazine. "We used to bring our friends up to New York and whoop it up."

New York City muso-art celebs the Talking Heads took note of the B-52's' special sounds, and an offer from their parent label Warner Bros. generated some ardent competition between several record companies. The band finally came home to roost in the W.B. coop.

Although people seemed sure that the B-52's would perform decently on the record racks, even the most optimistic were shocked when their self-titled debut album sold about 500,000 copies with zero mainstream airplay. (This was back before the industry began to take the independent college radio stations seriously, a condition that was altered by bands like the B's.)

"The B-52's' is an album of faith in the old axiom 'Rock 'n' roll won't change the world, but it can change your life,'" enthused Billy Altman in *Creem* magazine in 1979.

With the first blush of good fortune coloring their cheeks pink and their wallets green, the atomic band from Athens decided to relocate. In 1980, they jointly purchased a home in the town of Mahopac in upstate New York. Their comparison shopping time had been severely hampered by an impending Japanese tour, and they ended up with only three days to house hunt before they split for one tour after another.

Their second album, *Wild Planet*, definitely did not suffer from second-album syndrome. Many of the songs were conceived in the same sessions that spawned the first album. The material was strong and the B's' playing had tightened up in all the right places, honed by the months of one-nighters all over the world. The strength of numbers like "Private Idaho" pushed the album into the Billboard Top Twenty.

With the B-52's riding on top of the wild wave of international pop stardom, no one guessed that they were about to begin a long, painful wipeout.

One contributing factor was their surroundings. The house in Mahopac didn't exactly give the band the friendly, cozy environment they craved for work and play. "It was a big house, we had plenty of room, but it was like we were in exile . . ." Keith told Karen Schoemer of *Spin* magazine. Fred Schneider adds that it was " . . . more like a low-security institution with five inmates."

In addition, the neighbors were less than hospitable. Visions of earth-shaking parties and naked teenagers on drugs and a million other rock-star clichés probably danced in their tiny minds, so they devoted themselves to the expulsion of the potentially perverse upstarts. "We got sued for years by the next-door neighbors just because they didn't like men and women living together . . ." Cindy told *Spin* magazine. "It was really strange. They thought we were the evil plague coming down."

Meanwhile, the tastes of the world were undergoing some rather intense changes. People were discovering rap music and the wonderful world of MTV-assisted European synthesizer bands. When the umpteenth British invasion commenced, many indigenous stateside bands like the B's were trampled by rampaging redcoats whose hairstyles rivaled Kate and Cindy's wigs.

Third-album producer and Talking Head David Byrne was absorbed in his own projects and shelved recording for a while, so the B-52's put together *Party Mix*, a conglomeration of faves that didn't really dent the charts. When the Byrne-ed mini-platter "Mesopotamia" hit the racks, the hacks hit back. "Mesopotamia" crawled up to Number 35 on the Billboard Charts and fainted.

"Hey, I hate to be a party poop, but I think these guys might be running out of steam," Richard C. Walls wrote in a 1983 review of their fourth LP, *Whammy!* " . . . if you were one of those who was disappointed by 'Mesopotamia' 'cause you felt that David Byrne's techno-proficiency and au courant garnishing obscured the B's thrift shop eclecticism, you're in for another letdown here . . ." And only a couple of years before, hoary old rock stiff Robert Christgau had used the pages of the same magazine to dub the B-52's "the world's greatest new-wave kiddie-novelty disco-punk band."

Sick of wasting their time quibbling with nitpicking neighbors, the B's ditched the upstate digs in '83 and headed for the concrete jungle, New York City. They began recording *Bouncing Off the Satellites*. But external pressures were messing with the band's collective head. " . . . we were still friends, but we had been falling apart a

Halloween 1978 found the band opening the Mudd Club, it was about the fourth or fifth time the group had performed in N.Y.C. and bras and girdles were the costumes of the evening.

bit as a group," Fred told *Spin* magazine. Everyone began writing their own songs, instead of relying on their tried and true method of working things out through lengthy jam-fests. Then, before the album was completed, Ricky Wilson suddenly died of what was later reported to be AIDS-related cancer on October 12, 1985. Ricky had been diagnosed as suffering from cancer of the lymph nodes. He was thirty-two years old.

The death of their founding father was a tremendous shock to a band that had already experienced more than their share of bad karma. Ricky had always been the voice of their conscience, the originator of their unique guitar sound that utilized only specially open tuned strings. "I always considered Ricky as a teacher," Keith explained in *Spin* magazine. "I learned so much from him . . . He was always encouraging me to write, so I really depended on his criticism."

November 1, 1978 found David Bowie, Frank Zappa, and other celebs being entertained by this band from Planet Claire. This show at the Mudd Club was the last performance before they really "broke out."

C

Cindy was devastated by the loss of not only a friend and collaborator, but her big brother. "I adored my brother, he was more than a brother—he was a mentor. He was the coolest person alive. He had the greatest sense of humor and uniqueness about him. He really had a vision about him. He was one of the strongest elements of the B-52's in the beginning . . . He was everything."

"Ricky was our primary musical catalyst. After his death we decided not to tour because we couldn't imagine playing without him," Keith said in 1989.

Finishing the album without Ricky was a painful task, not the positive creative experience it should have been, and understandably the end result was weak. The fifth disc slipped out of the charts and the public ear after barely stirring up a ripple.

Years later, Kate looked back into the dark ages of the B-52's and told *B-Side* magazine, "We thought maybe that was the end—the natural end of the band. We had been together a long time. So when we started promoting *Bouncing Off the Satellites*, we decided not to tour because we couldn't replace Ricky."

Things went from bad to worse. Cindy admits that she fell apart, tortured by her grief and the constant reminders of her brother engendered by the burdens associated with dealing with his estate. She told *Rolling Stone*, "If it hadn't been for my husband . . . I'd have gone. I'd have killed myself or something." *Bouncing Off the Satellites* had been the band's most expensive project to date, and its commercial disaster-area status combined with the band's understandable refusal to tour meant no royalty or gig checks. "We really had to tighten our belts," Fred remembered in *Rolling Stone*. "We were just barely staying afloat, living off our catalog."

Although the B's had wisely put aside a certain amount of money as a "pension fund," they were cornered into raiding it to support themselves. Keith and Cindy sold their Manhattan home, and Kate soon followed, putting her apartment on the block. Her full-time man, Tim Rollins, who had been among the "select" audience at the first Max's gig, was doing all right and helped bridge the financial gap. Fred and artist Kenny Scharf put out an illustrated book of poetry. Keith retreated to an idyllic house near Woodstock in upstate New York near Kate's equally peaceful homestead and began to recuperate. The band saw each other, but they seemed to have hit the end of the dirty back road that had taken them to Planet Claire and back.

"Everybody relied on Ricky to make a lot of decisions. Once he was gone, they pulled through and started making decisions themselves," Robert Waldrop told *Rolling Stone*. At first, Keith penned a tune here or there. He turned to other forms of music besides rock for his listening fare, evolving a new frame of reference incorporating everything from new-age music to the blues. Kate and Cindy visited and he played the resulting

tunes for them, one of which was the mainstay of *Cosmic Thing*'s third single, "The Deadbeat Club," an autobiographical anthem about their lazy days in Athens, sipping coffee and hanging loose.

"We would meet sporadically at first," said Kate in *B-Side* magazine. "Once a week or twice a week but then we started really getting into the groove. We got a rehearsal studio and a regular schedule and got it going."

Eventually, the B-52's began to regain their sense of purpose, leaving their management behind in favor of new blood and changing polo ponies midstream for Warner Bros. subsidiary Reprise. Keith abandoned his drum kit and took up the guitar. "I wanted to keep some connection with what Ricky had done," he explained to Michael Azzerad. "He was a very key ingredient in our sound, and I just didn't want that to disappear."

And it didn't, and neither did the B-52's. After recording the title track of their soon-to-be best-selling LP to date with superstar producer Nile Rodgers for the soundtrack of Julien Temple's *Earth Girls Are Easy*, they

New York City debut at Max's Kansas City. He
hasn't begun to think about the long ride back
to Athens in their Volkswagen "bug."

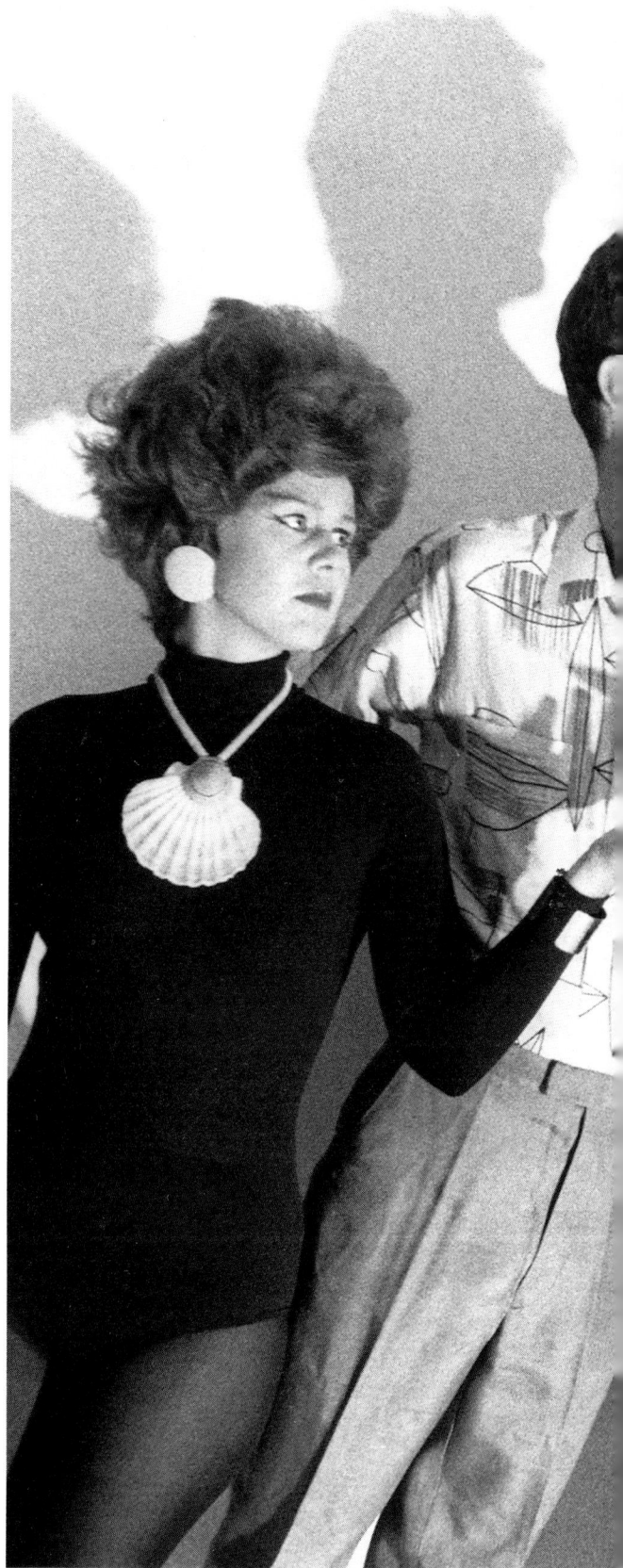

held their breath and signed up for the long march. They committed to an album produced by Mr. Rodgers and the equally accomplished Don Was, who had a special respect for their sound, calling it "a folk music indigenous to an exotic land."

"We unanimously agreed that we wanted to have fun with this record and not worry about what was on the radio or what was current," Keith said.

The result was a *Cosmic Thing* that gave birth to a new B-52's, with a multiplatinum album and more than one Top Five single. With "Love Shack" and "Roam" selling like the proverbial hotcakes from Hades, the band has finally reached the heights, and they've utilized their success wisely to benefit causes they strongly believe in. Their support tour for *Cosmic Thing* included information and registration booths for spokespersons from PETA (People for the Ethical Treatment of Animals), Greenpeace, and Amnesty International. They've

"Thrift shop chic" was practically invented by
this innovative band. The toy piano was
actually used for several of their first shows.

achieved a perspective, a sense of purpose, and a chance to fuse a bond with fans by giving something back to the world that has given them so much. But then, giving back what they receive has always been the most important part of the B-52's' philosophy.

"They worked out a lot of grief through joy," Robert Waldrop concluded in *Rolling Stone* in early 1990. "You know those funerals down there in New Orleans where everybody's just waving umbrellas and playing jazz? I think this record was kind of like that."